T0010540

SEE Noah's Ark Biodiversity Conservation Book Series

The Yunnan
Snub-Nosed Monkey

Written by Zhong Tai and Liu Liyun   Illustrated by Bai Song and Xia Tian

SEE Noah's Ark Biodiversity Conservation Book Series

Editorial Committee:

Chief Editor: Xiao Jin

Associate Editor: Liu Liyun

Member of Editorial Board: Xia Tian, Su Yusong, Yu Luyao

Member of Advisory Board: Yang Yuming, Zhang Li, Han Lianxian, Sun Weibang, Xie Hongfang, Ye Ming

Copy Editor: Xiao Jin, Liu Liyun, Chen Jinsou

Layout Design: Kunming Benpu Culture Communication Co., Ltd

Invited Consultant: Ma Junling

Cooperation Partner:

SEE Foundation

APSA

Nie Er and National Anthem Culture Education Base, XI-SHAN District, Kunming

Preface

The Southwest Project Center of the Alashan Society of Entrepreneurs & Ecology (SEE) initiated a program in 2013 for biodiversity conservation of the alpine forests in China's mountainous Southwest. Named SEE Noah's Ark, it is financed by the SEE Foundation in Beijing. Multiple conservation projects have been implemented by working with various stakeholders to protect endangered and rare species of flora and fauna, especially those with extremely small populations. It adopts solutions inspired by nature and advocates participation by the community, encouraging protection and the sustainable use of local biological resources.

The stories in the SEE book series: *The Asian Elephant*, *The Yunnan Snub-Nosed Monkey*, *The Green Peafowl*, *The Fish of the Jinsha River*, and *The Himalayan Honeybee*, all come from true experiences of front-line rangers and locals in conservation action. They are incredible. For both nature's characters and the people in the story, their connection to the native land and affection towards each other is rarely heard and miraculous in their own way. We then came up with a proposal to compile these lovely stories in a picture book to all our friends who have supported SEE conservation projects. They can be linked to real characters from dense woods and remote mountains, where heart touching stories occurred due to their generous support.

This picture book series is a group of works by conservation workers, scientists, sociologists, writers, and artists. The characters, environment, and neighboring creatures have all been carefully selected from real situations in our projects. In addition, explanatory notes of conservation are made to enrich the reading experience. We hope you enjoy it!

We extend our respects to those who have worked so hard to conserve their natural homeland, as well as to the SEE members and public who give donations to support these projects. These volumes are our gifts for the United Nations Biodiversity Conference COP15 held in Kunming.

XIAO JIN
Secretary of the SEE's Southwest Project Center
Chairperson of the SEE Noah's Ark Committee
June 2021

Data File: Yunnan Snub-Nosed Monkey

Name in Chinese	滇金丝猴 (DIANJINSIHOU)
Name in English	Black-and-white snub-nosed monkey
Alternate Names	Snub-Nosed monkey, black-gold monkey, Black-And-White Snub-Nosed Monkey
Latin Name	Rhinopithecus bieti
Kingdom	Animalia
Phylum	Chordata
Subphylum	Vertebrate
Class	Mammalia

Subclass	Haplorhini
Order	Simiiformes
Family	Cercopithecidae
Genus	Rhinopithecus
Species	Black-and-white snub-nosed monkey
Subspecies	No subspecies
Distribution	Yunnan, Tibet
Authorship	Milne-Edwards, 1897
Conservation Status	Endangered

Black-and-white snub-nosed monkey Distribution and Established Conservation Areas

Province/ City	County/ District	Conservation Areas and National Parks Constructed
Yunnan	Dêqên County	Yunnan Baima Snow Mountain Nature Reserves
	Weixi County	
	Gucheng District	Laojunshan National Park, Yulong County Shitou Town Black-and-white snub-nosed monkey Patrol Squad
	Lanping County	Yunling Provincial Nature Reserve
	Yunlong County	Yunnan Yunlong Tianchi National Nature Reserve Management Office
Tibet	Markam County	Tibet Markam County Yunnan Sub-nosed Monkey National Nature Reserve

Note: Black-and-white Snub-nosed Monkey is the standard expression in English, distinguished from the Black Snub-nosed Monkey discovered later along the Salween River during 2008–2010.

The huge alpine Snow Mountain, covered by white snow in winter, is vibrant with forest beings. Uncle Yu from the patrol squad, a member of the Lisu ethnicity, lives with his family and neighbors at the Rumbling Drum Valley Bamboos, at the foothill of the mountain.

One day, out on patrol, Uncle Yu found a wounded black-and-white snub-nosed monkey. When he saw the little snub-nosed monkey, startled and in pain, he felt like his own child suffering. He carried the creature back to the Wildlife Rescue Station.

Golden Pheasant

3

Around the habitats of the black-and-white snub-nosed monkey in the Snow mountains are mostly Tibetans, Lisu, and Yi people with pasturing traditions. There are also Naxi and Bai people who work the land for their livelihoods. They believe in the sacred nature of the mountains, naming the monkeys which never disturb their peace, and live together with the mountain god, "white monkeys" or "black monkeys." In their ethnic legend, they believe the black-and-white snub-nosed monkey is their ancestor and remains their relative. Since the monkeys are messengers, living with the mountain god, these people have been on friendly terms with them throughout the generations.

The Yunnan Snub-Nosed Monkey

Luo Ya, Director of the Rescue Station, cleaned and stitched up the little monkey's wound. Every day, Old Yu picked fresh lichens and young leaves from the broad-leaf trees to feed the monkey. The creature had dark eyes and a cute face that inspires love and sympathy. Everybody called it Ling Ling (Smarty).

4

Ling Ling's wound healed up quickly. It must be about time to send him back to the mountain.

But the patrol squad couldn't bear to be parted from Ling Ling. As soon as they reached the edge of the woods, Ling Ling leaped excitedly onto a branch ... but then suddenly rushed back and buried himself in Old Shu's arms. So, he had feelings for them too!

5

The Baima Snow Mountain National Nature Reserve is the largest black-and-white snub-nosed monkey conservation site in China. Inside the reserve, the conservation targets the coniferous forests, mountain vegitatian along vertical belts of the lactlscaoe, and the black-and-white snub-nosed monkey. The reserves are located in Dégén County and Weixi County in northwest Yunnan and Tibetan Autonomous Prefecture. The Tacheng Wildlife Rescue Station is at the southernmost tip of Weixi Reserve Management Branch. Established in 2010, its goal is to look after the black-and-white snub-nosed monkey community in the Rumbling Drum Valley, providing support and medical assistance.

The Yunnan Snub-Nosed Monkey

Ling Ling roamed the forest for two days before he finally found his family. Monkey Mama held Ling Ling in a welcoming embrace when she saw him, kissing him over and over. Several of Ling Ling's aunties came over to smooch his little face. Ling Ling's little brother was overjoyed to have him back as well. He ran over to Monkey Mama and they started playing.

6

Ling Ling

Seeing Ling Ling reunited with his family, Luo Ya and Old Yu, following behind for all this time, breathed a sigh of relief.

Sooty-headed Bulbul

7

The Yunnan Snub-Nosed Monkey

The black-and-white snub-nosed monkey troop has a two-layered social structure, consisting of multiple One Male Unit family groups and a minimum of one All Male Units. Family groups are mostly polygamous, with units made up of one adult male, two or more adult females, and their offspring. This adult male is known as the dominant figure (alpha male). Black-and-white snub-nosed monkey babies are cared for collectively by the females.

Ling Ling was back with his companions. He'd got his happy life back. Every day he played and toyed around. He didn't have a care in the world.

8

But the good days didn't last long. Monkey Papa gave Ling Ling his evacuation orders. No mercy. He was to leave and go far away.

Ling Ling felt wronged and scared. He and the other single monkeys lingered in the forest for a few days – before they just had to rush back and find Mom.

Monkey Papa wouldn't soften up. Not a few days later, he snarled and growled to drive Ling Ling off again. Back and forth it went, more than once, before Ling Ling figured out what was going on, so he finally stuck to his All Male Unit. Without Mama to look after him now, newcomers were always teased and bullied by the elder monkeys. Ling Ling was lucky to still have two or three young monkeys about his size, starting their bachelor's journey together.

Ling Ling

Musk Deer

The Yunnan Snub-Nosed Monkey

The male leaves its natal breeding family at the age of 3–4 to join an All Male Unit. This "singles club" consists of kicked-out or elderly males, expelled from mating battles as well as juvenile or young monkeys who have left the family unit and not yet earned mating credentials.

Ling Ling

Owl

Life was not easy in the All Male Unit. Ling Ling had to find his own food to stay full. He had to learn the habits of the larger males and stay away from their feeding territory, in order to avoid being beaten!

As a young male monkey, Ling Ling learned to compete to get everything he wanted. He'll be fighting for his entire life – death alone will be the end of it. Every day he swang through the trees, working hard on his fighting skills. He had two friends of the same age – Nan Nan and Kun Kun. They went around together, and looked after one another, like the Three Musketeers of this All Male Unit.

Chinese goral

Ling Ling

The Yunnan Snub-Nosed Monkey

The male pecking order is crucial for these monkeys, not only for keeping their families and determining their own position, but also for family status within the entire group. It is through physical strength that the individual determines his role in the All Male Unit. Seniority and physical size determine the ranks, with those of the same rank separated by fighting ability.

Punk

12

More than four years flew by. Ling Ling has now grown into a
mature male, handsome and massive. He has reached mating age as well.
Now that he had seen those imperious males with their harems, and their
sons and daughters, Ling Ling wanted to escape from being single
and was eager to lead his own females. He began to make plans to
challenge the Alpha Male.

The Three Musketeers set their sights on Punk, heading a family of
four females and two girls. One of his hands was crippled. They
reckoned he'd be an easy target. They'd get what they wanted
with ease.

But it was not easy! Maybe they were inexperienced – but fierce Punk ame crashing towards them. He combined ingle punches and flying kicks, sending them hurling into the trees and scattering.

Punk

Blood Pheasant

Ling Ling

13

The Yunnan Snub-Nosed Monkey

The male enters breeding maturity at around seven years of age. Because of the polygamous family structure, female monkeys are objects of competition, and they can only be occupied by the primary male. Obtaining an alpha male position requires a male to challenge a family alpha male and win the battle, almost the only opportunity to secure his mating position.

Ling Ling worked out even harder every day once the wounds were healed. He was preparing for the next battle.

This time the Three Musketeers would focus on Punk's nap time. They started a surprise attack from three fronts, all at once. Punk fell out of the tree and was badly injured. He lay still on the ground. As the night came, he retreated and slunk away.

Nan Nan

Ling Ling

Kun Kun

Punk

The black-and-white snub-nosed monkey spends most of its time in the trees. Groups choose relatively lofty trunks to sleep in at night, to avoid natural predators and bad weather. Males occupy the inner layers of the tree crown, nearer the trunk or where there is more food, while females and adolescents search for food in the highest and external layers. When they collect ground food or go on a group migration, they would most claw the ground.

The Yunnan Snub-Nosed Monkey

Ling Ling snatched two of Punk's females, taking a farewell to his single life and becoming an alpha male of a new family. The brave Nan Nan and fierce Kun Kun also had their own families, each with one female from Punk's family.

Wife 1 (Liu Chun)

Wife 2 (San Mi)

Ling Ling

15

The first winter for Ling Ling as an alpha male was extremely cold. The snow blew madly about for more than three months straight. They had eaten all the dried fruits on the trees – only lichens and fir buds remained.

In the bitter cold, Ling Ling was losing weight. Yet his sense of family responsibility grew stronger. Whenever he found food, he always guarded it at some high spot, keeping hold of his territory, letting the females eat first – they had already carried his offspring.

As spring came, the two wives gave Ling Ling two baby monkeys. Finally, Ling Ling was now a dad!

Wife 1 (Liu Chun)

Wife 2 (San Mi)

17

The black-and-white snub-nosed monkey's primary diet includes the tender leaves or buds from the fir and pine trees and also lichens. This is mostly a plant-based diet. The monkeys must spend most of the day eating to make up for low nutrition levels and then take long pauses for digestion. The black-and-white snub-nosed monkey will reduce activity, so as to conserve energy in the food-scarce winter.

The Yunnan Snub-Nosed Monkey

Imperial woodpecker

Wife 4

Five years later, Ling Ling's outstanding bravery won the heart of the other two females. But it also aroused jealousy in those from the All Male Unit and provoked other family heads. Ling Ling only wanted more females and more babies.

Nan Nan and Kun Kun weren't his friends anymore. Nowadays, they were his rivals – always keeping a close guard on their own family.

18

Wild wolf

Wife 1 (Liu Chun)

Ling Ling fought the alpha male Black-Hair in a mortal battle over the next two months. Finally, one of Black-Hair's wives felt his strength vanishing, and defected to Ling Ling through her own choice. Now with five females in his family, Ling Ling led the largest family amongst the monkey groups in Rumbling Drum Valley.

Wife 2 (San Mi)

Wife 3

Ling Ling

The Yunnan Snub-Nosed Monkey

For the black-and-white snub-nosed species, there is no single male monkey king to dominate all females, though clear rankings do exist. The highest-ranked male will be the alpha male who leads the largest number of females in its family. The family will also take priority in food and rest position.

Ling Ling's dad

Ling Ling's mom

Ling Ling's aunt

In March of the following year, the first new shoots arrived in Rumbling Drum Valleys, Ling Ling had another two new babies.

Ling Ling recalled the days when his dad was sitting on the tree in a royal manner and overlooking his territories. Now, Ling Ling has won his own kingdom, having written his own legend, all through his own hard work and ability to fight.

The black-and-white snub-nosed monkey would usually have one pregnancy every two years. Pregnancy takes seven months. Baby monkeys are often born around March or April, when the climate is becoming moderate, food is plentiful, and survival rates are high.

The Yunnan Snub-Nosed Monkey

21

About the Authors

Zhong Tai (Tibetan Chinese) is the deputy director of the Administration and Protection Bureau of Baima Snow Mountain National Nature Reserve in Yunnan and the deputy director of Yunnan Snub-Nosed Monkey Research Center. In the thirty-eight years after the establishment of the Nature Reserve, he has worked there as a frontline patrolman, community co-management explorer, wildlife researcher, protection manager, etc. As a pioneer who cooperated with scientific research institutes in Yunnan's snub-nosed monkey fieldwork, he has participated in all the developmental stages of Yunnan's snub-nosed monkey study and protection.

Liu Liyun is an advisor at the SEE Project Center. She has provided consulting services for the project planning and development of the Center, and she was in charge of summarizing report text, building and guiding staff capacity, planning external publicity, etc.

About the Illustrators

Bai Song has a Master's degree in engineering and has engaged in art education work for many years. She is now vice president and professional leader of Yunnan Light and Textile Industry Vocational Collage. She has edited and published two national planning textbooks, one jewelry major series teaching material for vocational institutes, and many educational, teaching, and research-related papers in relevant academic journals.

Xia Tian received his bachelor's degree in costume design from Yunnan Arts University and his master's degree in information technology engineering from Wuhan University. In addition, he has studied visual communication at Tongji University. He is the founder and general manager of Kunming Benpu Culture Communication Co., Ltd. and an external tutor at Yunnan University of Finance and Economics.

SEE Noah's Ark Biodiversity Conservation Book Series

SEE: The Yunnan Snub-Nosed Monkey

Written by Zhong Tai and Liu Liyun
Illustrated by Bai Song and Xia Tian

First published in 2023 by Royal Collins Publishing Group Inc.
Groupe Publication Royal Collins Inc.
BKM Royalcollins Publishers Private Limited

Headquarters: 550-555 boul. René-Lévesque O Montréal (Québec) H2Z1B1 Canada
India office: 805 Hemkunt House, 8th Floor, Rajendra Place, New Delhi 110 008

Original Edition © Yunnan Science & Technology Press Co., Ltd.

All rights reserved. Without limiting the rights under copyright reserved above, no part of this publication may be reproduced, stored in or introduced into a retrieval system, or transmitted in any form or by any means (electronic, mechanical, photocopying, recording or otherwise), without the prior written permission of both the copyright owner and the above publisher of this book.

ISBN: 978-1-4878-1082-5

To find out more about our publications, please visit www.royalcollins.com.